The Fools Guide to the Perfect Life: Print Book

Jack R Ernest

Copyright

First Printing: December 2022

IBSN: 978-1-4710-1814-5

Essay One

Introduction

What is a man without his mind? The mind is the ingredient behind the Eiffel Tower, the Hubble Space Telescope, General relativity, Chopin's Nocturnes, love and life itself. The mind is man. It is what has given us the advantage over our fellow species that inhabit this awesome blue planet. Our mind, with its neurons and synapses combusting can let us dream and man through dreaming can see back in time and into the future. The animal has no such gift. The animal must concern itself only about food and survival. It cannot fathom existence like its fearsome predator can. The animal sees the blue skies and the dawning of the darkness and consequently adjusts its life to this astronomical rhythm. A man can see into the atom and he sees far back into the birth of time. And yet he cannot distinguish himself living on this planet in the twenty first century. Despite his luxury of self-awareness he is as blind as the animal when it comes to self-perception. Even with the tool of language man is chained by his own lack of insight into his own condition. Conformity is the gravity of civilization it must be asserted. This invisible force has shaped the cause of man just as the waves mould the shoreline of a country. This is the faceless field that has given society its motivation to exist. We cannot see it or feel it and yet we are condemned to heed to it. We bow to the will of conformity unconsciously. We are moral, we love and we live on unconscious instinct. We may as well be an animal that cannot speak or dream because we fail to take advantage of our tool of language. The masses live lives of quiet desperation. They are induced to bend to the will of society rather than forge their own being. Free will is an illusion. Conformism has man in a straitjacket. Man suffers no autonomy even in the age of reason. Much like a star is moulded into a spherical shape by the forces acting in aggregation around it; man is moulded by the eyes of others so much that he forgoes his sovereignty in exchange for acceptance. Life becomes a pseudo-popularity contest. We live to gain image and status wise and not to please ourselves. Any fortitude of existence is strengthened when we are held in high regard by our peers. As such we live to make others happy at the expense of our own personal happiness. The eyes of others shape our destiny. Our daily refuge is plagued by the sentiments of others and we live to pacify their will. This essay is an attempt to convey the meaning of Existential Nihilism. Existential Nihilism can provoke feelings of anguish or one can find their liberty in it. It all depends on how one interprets the philosophy.

1

We endure but we are not alive. We are not acquainted with ourselves as we live. This is the price of addiction. We discharge ourselves into life at the expense of realizing that we are alive. The unconscious mind cannot indulge self-awareness. It considers it a disease even in this day and age. As such men and women alike have no pertinence on their existence. They wake up and go to work; they then come home and go to sleep; they then repeat this formula for the duration of their existence. They are brain dead or drip fed their day to day gratuity. The essence of life has long perished in their barren practise. Their unconscious mind has them automated to live day to day like cattle in a field. The conscience then aligns itself to addictions to attempt to defeat the existential angst that it has awoken. We are unconsciously living and not by our own conscious right of way. Men are infatuated with success as are women. They both want to be deemed socially respectable and this desire has poisoned their way of life. They live on a paralysed instinct. This endeavours to devise them in the same scheme as their competitor. We are all the same. There is no disparity between us.

Boredom is the origin of all our woes. Rewind the dominos of genius and destruction and the first domino to fall is always a poor tolerance of boredom. Man is incapable of sitting alone quietly in a room for an extended period of time. He must be active. His mind becomes disorientated when left to its own devices. It yearns to feel intoxicated in escape. The choice in life is: Boredom and everything else. Is one able to accept their ennui? If not, their mind will attempt to alleviate the situation. Thus man pours himself into the various escapes of life. Conversation and television, art and alcohol, regardless of what it is, they all provide a means to escape the demons that life gives birth too. The existential angst is kept bereft of man if his mind is busy. We dive head first into the arms of the divine so we can have meaning in a meaningless existence. This is why marriage becomes the standard of existence. We waste our souls on serving its will purely so we can pass the time. Life unfortunately is existentially redundant. There is no meaning to existence and this is the core truth that we cannot bear.

Our identity serves to give us a more self-absorbed view of ourselves in the world than we ordinarily should. Our identity is our name, face, personality and what others see in us. These four qualities displayed are used as a source of recognition for others. We can use reason through language and this coupled with our identity, means we foster an ego centric view of mankind in the universe. We invariably put ourselves on a higher pedestal than our fellow animal species. So many men and women found their esteem on the basis that they are diverse from other species of animals. They hold their views as such because they unconsciously presuppose that they are disparate through reason and identity. Life thus becomes about image and success. The greater universe lies undiscovered and invalidated. People see life as getting up in the morning and relaxing in the evening. The stars, the sun, the other planets may as well not prevail because people do not acknowledge them.

To alter one's life, one does not need a complete renovation of their day to day activities. In order for one to improve their existence, they just need to rectify their perception. Life is what you perceive it to be. You can bask in the sunshine and dance in the rain. It all depends on how you view this gift you have been allocated. People automatically fall into the trap of conformism in that they are told that they must be doing A, B and C to be happy in life. This is the lie that we have unconsciously come to endorse as final. The powers that be say we can't be happy until we have conquered in life. In effect our daily existence becomes about the destination and not the journey. But the only happiness one finds at the destination is the happiness they brought through the journey. On this premise, in order for one to be content in the future they must be happy in the present and the means to be happy now is to be grateful for just existing. People are deceived, for having a life is not enough by their standards. They must have a more grand life. This is a toxic way of thinking for it places emphasis on gratification over gratitude. Change your perception of what is happiness. Be grateful for just having the ability to be alive. Your existence is your genius.

We are hysterical beings and in so much as being the reason why we live, it is also the reason why we fall foul of pain and hurt in life. Life is not enough; we wish to feel alive. Emotion is what we call feeling alive, but akin to any addict we become desperate to feel our high. In want of feeling amorous and fulfilled, we let ourselves be emotionally beguiled by various qualities of day to day life. We seek out relationships and follow sports teams because we have an emotional void that needs to be filled. People thus live on emotion and as such fail to recognise themselves as they live. If one can observe how they live and why they live they can then change the how and why they live. But they first must see and only when they do see can they act. Self-discovery is only found when one looks inwards. One can look to the world for change, but only the individual can change the world.

We are all following in life. We hound sports teams or famous people and that is how they make their money. But has one ever asked why they follow? Why do we do what everyone else does? Is it conscious or is it unconscious? The reason being is that the relationship, the sports team and the politician all enable us to feel dynamic and that is why we are obligated to follow unconsciously. A consequence of following is that we unconsciously become obsessed with image. We involuntarily enter a shallow rat race of desirability and we do it on impulse. We do not realize that we follow but rather we only realize the consequences of our following. One thus brings upon them wave after wave of anxieties because they fail to meet the requirements of what is requested of them through implicit conformity. What happens is that we wake up in retirement and realize we have exhausted our existence for a race.

We are so infatuated with life that we cease to observe ourselves living. We eternally live on instinct and perhaps fail on it also. Life has a habit of blinding ourselves to ourselves. As we partake in the various qualities of existence we discount our ability to observe ourselves as we live. Take for instance a conversation between two people: PERSON A (PA) talks to PERSON B (PB). So (PA) says something to which (PB) responds and then (PA) responds to (PB) initial response. As such both people become delirious on each other and both are discombobulated to their own being. Our existence is just a response to an initial response. Our whole lives are a reaction to a preceding action. The fabric of our lives is built out of reactions be they verbal or physical. Consequently very few humans are self-acquainted of themselves as they negotiate life. They are governed by pure conformist proclivity. Ones liberty and thus self-improvement can only be found in their self-awareness. Become more self-knowledgeable about how you live and then you can determine how you live. One cannot alter themselves unless they know what they have to change. A lot of our persona is unconsciously controlled and henceforth to transform one's self means to retrain ones unconscious to react differently.

The multitudes of men and women conform and do so on instinct. We are programmed from childhood to behave in a precise fashion. Why does everyone feel the need to work and be in relationships? Why does a relationship consist of a convenient two people? Why not three people or seven? Conformity has become the criteria by which people persevere through life. It is not right nor is it wrong but it is a model which has been adopted by society. Conformity is extoled because it is the system by which the world operates. People get lectured on how to live, they then adopt the method and they furthermore seek justification for this prescription of living. Consequently we are impinged with media propaganda pertaining towards conformism because we unconsciously seek rationalization for wasting our existence. So men see advertisements that advertise marriage and work and women see magazines that preach about the value of relationships and families. The will to conform is almost congenital in nature. We observe what we see when we grow up and unconsciously embrace the system. We think we are living by our own free will but it has been predetermined long before we mellow how we will live. Furthermore we are under social duress to accomplish in life from friends and family. This stress also covertly makes us bend to the will of conformity. We conform implicitly.

A financial mortgage puts us in a dilemma with regards our money and also our careers. That we have to pay back a loan means we must work and must pump our cash into the loan. What people don't realize is that our friends and family also have us in a bind. This bind is a psychological mortgage. The very people one turns towards for support are the very people who restrict our freedom. We fear above all else bringing dishonour to our friends and family. We dread a negative judgement from them. To inspire our friends we must adhere to certain parameters. We must conduct ourselves in a certain way or else they become agitated with us. Very often we are instructed to marry and to work because we are under invisible tension from friends and family to do so. Furthermore, if our friends and family are married and in employment we feel abandoned. As long as one puts emphasis on friendship and family they will be oppressed. Freedom resonates from within and in being who you wish to be, despite the murmurings of the herd. To become liberated one must elude the majority.

From a young age we are engulfed with what is deemed the correct way to live. The conformist propaganda is relentless and our unconscious mind is bombarded daily with it. We thus become idealist dreamers who yearn for a greater life than the one we already possess. People attest that when they are married they will be happy. They assume that when they have the right job they will be content. Our lives become commoditized in that we treat them as objects that need to taste the honey of success to be justified. Life doesn't toil like this though. The ideal life is the one you have now. The only happiness one will find at the end of the road is the happiness they import with them on the road. We are drugged on the idealistic "good life." We think that it will reward us down the line. Consequently we rebuff living in the present on the certainty that we will live in the future.

Envy is a subtle flattery. People fail to see that if they are resentful of another individual it is because that individual retains something superior. Because of the shallow rat race that is materialism, we unconsciously compare and contrast ourselves to other people. Those who are inferior we do not fear, but those who we deem superior we come to detest. Capitalism has us dazed in our pursuit of success so much that if we are not number one we equate ourselves with failure. Jealousy degrades so many in the competitive world. So many lives are existentially leaked on the race to be better than the other. The rat race is unreservedly consuming on the twenty first century man. He pours his time and mind into becoming better than his peers. So much in fact that he renounces who he is now in favour of who he will be in the future. But if one is not happy with who they are at sunset, they will not be happy come the sunrise.

If one wishes to be happy then just be happy. It is that simple. The capitalist ethos has one polluted insofar as happiness is an entity that must be acquired. We get lectured that we cannot be happy until we have accomplished in life. We frequently tell ourselves that our future lies in materialism and what it entails. We relate to ourselves this so much consciously, that it becomes imprinted into our unconscious mind and thus we see no other means to live. We must be provoked from this poisoned way of thought. People must be schooled on how lucky they are to exist. It all starts through altering ones perception of what is life. We are programmed to see it as being desirable and thus wager our happiness on this. Thus when man miscarries with regards the standard that is demanded he becomes melancholic. One must modify their perception of life to appreciate their existence. Think of the universe, think of the atoms that constitute your body and think about how fortunate you are to be able to exist.

Language is the light of civilization. Without the ability to speak man is defunct. This is ultimately what separates us from other animals. That we can use language to navigate through life's choppy straits serves to embellish our existence over other species. Unfortunately every positive has a negative. We become addicted to conversation. We need to be cherished by it. Our lives come to revolve around articulation. Language has conditioned us to talk when we should think. People thus expend large amounts of energy and time talking instead of logically thinking. Through concise articulation one becomes a prostitute of conformity. Through being engaged with others and their language we sell ourselves and rarely question what we do. Language gives birth to all these concepts that we endeavour to follow unconsciously and one must be aware of how one is swindled by the very thing that makes life what it is.

Man must be entertained in life. Life is an addiction of which entertainment provides the essence. We cannot handle being bored and because of this we venture into the real world to relieve ourselves of this ennui. All facets of life serve to enrapture man. Conversation, relationships, books, films, sports teams, food etc. They all strive to gratify man. The means may be different, but the end is the same: enjoyment. A problem occurs unconsciously however in that we request to be intrigued at all times. This means we look to the world and tell it to placate our existence and this is done on impulse. We are addicts of a ritual existence. Simple existence is not enough for us for we need emotional justification for living. Consequently when we don't get our high from life we feel downcast.

Happiness cannot be bought, earned or traded. Happiness stems from within our souls. One can look to the future and attest that they will be content, but rarely does it come to fruition. That we are addicts of existence we actively seek reward from life in the form of gratified happiness. This is a happiness that is derived from success in the external world. So when an individual prevails in some way or form in life they feel emotionally content. But the feeling always dissipates and when it does a new addiction is sought. Pure happiness is the happiness one is endowed with from just existing and it is a happiness that cannot be taken from you. To exist in this hazardous world is the greatest celebration of one's life. To be able to wake up and taste the cool air is the triumph but many cannot see this. We are so programmed on external gratification that we cannot see the truth: That one's existence alone is their victory.

Man is contaminated by image. His life revolves around a daily cycle of harbouring the best image possible that he can represent. Economies function on this invisible necessity which people are slaves to. Why does a man drive a car worth one hundred thousand when a car that is worth ten times less would suffice? Why does a woman spend a fortune on a dress when a cheaper one would suffice? Both of them are ushered into spending vast sums of money in order to cultivate their image that they advertise to the greater world. A stellar image means they will be wanted and being wanted means they feel good. They are servants of addiction and nothing more. So long as one is absorbed in this contest to have the most rewarding image one can never be free because image demands more and more. The individual may improve their image but the potency wears off and a new improvement is deemed necessary. This is systematic of what psychologists call addiction, only this addiction is ascertained to be normal.

In life we retain these hidden standards of which someone must meet in order to be deemed attractive. This coupled with our childhood education serves to make us seek certain traits in people in order for us to emotionally respond to them. This indoctrination when young means we use the barometer of conversation to judge someone. Henceforth politicians and sales representatives make much effort to speak well purely because it taps into the unconscious mind of the individual. Alas we use this threshold as a means to separate people in our lives also. Those who speak with clarity are held in higher regard than those who don't and as such we get deceived by those who are considered ample speakers. Conversation is such a mainstay of daily existence that we forget how much power it possesses. We take it for granted. My advice is judge a person on merit and not how they articulate.

Life is a pseudo-popularity contest. From adolescence we are habituated to want to be in the most demand. Males wish to be coveted by the female and the female wishes to be anticipated by the male. As such we expend large amounts of time and emotion engaged in this tournament. Life thus becomes in effect a race to be the most endorsed. A psychological bubble is formed wherein the people compete against one another to attain the most, but the happiness that is earned is only provisional in nature. One becomes comforted when in high demand, but the drug wears off and the individual must seek the demand again. Treating life as a popularity contest will never deliver satisfaction. It will give little snippets of happiness but it is an addictive happiness that subsides after a while. Escaping the grasp of this style of living is vital to pure happiness. Pure happiness is the only war worth fighting for. If people are taught to engage in popularity contests unconsciously, they can be taught not to as well.

Only the individual can alter themselves. Success is perspiration and not inspiration. Reading self-help books or watching inspirational programmes makes us feel good emotionally, but the emotion, whatever it is, subsides. We wait for the world to shift us when we must shift our world. People's unconscious is plagued with the demons of capitalistic desire so much that they see no other existence. In trying to obtain happiness they delve deeper into the abyss. They try to placate capitalism at the expense of pure happiness. They read books that tell them to think positively and work hard that only fuel the greed that capitalism espouses. Change involves cultivation of ones unconscious to instinctively respond to life differently and it takes time. It is not enough to say consciously you will adjust, for one must condition their unconscious to see the world in a new shade. The good life is not material. The good life is perception. Existence itself is the greatest glory of life. Do not exhaust it all in want of a better one.

We know what we want from life. We want to work and marry. We want to enjoy ourselves at the weekends. We want a few laughs. People know what they want from life but they are clueless to why they want these things. The "what" is determined by the unconscious mind and not by conscious reason. But people are impervious to this subtle truth for they think they are consciously in command of their existence. Man consequently is not free. Far from it, he is subordinate to conformity, for that is what puts pressure on him with regards how to navigate through life. People thus bang the drum repetitively expecting the winds of change to blow them towards a new island of fortune. They repeat the same failings day after day and cannot comprehend why their existence stays the same. To revolutionize one's life one must first understand why they choose. Through acknowledgement of their decision process they can then train their unconscious to perceive life differently.

The existential strain of thought can be an axe or it can be an escape. If man is taught to be twenty first century man through education he can be taught to be existential in soul through his own self. Nihilism for the world can help man flee his suffering. In order for man to obtain his liberty in this world, he must rebel against the unconscious Will to Conform. He must see that the nihilism can be a release in this world. Life according to the existential nihilist is rudderless. Men are conditioned to see the meaning of life is sexual gratification and women are conditioned to see the meaning of life is relationships. But they are programmed through childhood indoctrination to believe these things. Success then is being prepared to challenge these rituals. Instead of seeking happiness from the external world, man can be instructed to seek happiness from within. Man's salvation lies within.

Has anyone ever wondered why the world just is? Has anyone ever questioned why billions of people all follow the same routine? It begs the question: What manipulates us psychologically that we all are prepared to mimic the same pattern? The answer is simple: Childhood indoctrination through education. Through being educated man is deprived of his freedom and is transformed into a machine. This machine is identical to all other machines in terms of actions and wants. Education manufactures our brains in such a way that we all chase the same passions in life. We want to work and marry only because we have been automated to do so from childhood. It is not coincidence that the world of eight billion people behaves the way it does. There is substance behind the façade. When young we believed anything. We believed in the tooth fairy and Santa Claus. As we age we realize they are fallacies. But when we were young we were also indoctrinated with the cult of conformism only we never grow up to realize it is a lie. We grow up to believe there is no other way to live, other than conforming to principles. When we do find out its more than likely too late. We are old and grey and the better part of our existence has passed by. Education teaches us to become reliant on each other. It tutors us to work for reward. It disciplines us to think alike rather than critically think as an individual. We are each nothing because we are inculcated to each be nothing and to enjoy this nothingness. Find your own voice before you grow old and lose it altogether. You achieve far more in life by being who you are and never letting others choose who you are.

Capitalism is the plague of the western world. Through its ethos men and women suffer daily and dissolve their existence and happiness on a chance that they will be happy in the future. The capitalist mentality has been learned through childhood. It then becomes unconsciously glued to the individuals psyche and they know of no other means to live. It tells the masses that they cannot be happy until they have triumphed in life. This happiness is dependent on success to be realized. The individuals thus live their daily lives in a state of competition with themselves. They cannot be content unless they have gained in some way or form. Capitalism is the arch nemesis of Buddhism. Buddhism instructs man to just be happy to be alive. Capitalism preaches that existence is not enough and one must succeed to live. It is a psychological disease that infects its host when young like a virus that taints ones vision and the ability to reason. One can never be happy in capitalism, for the success is short lived and must be repeated. Every day is a struggle under its shadow. But if man can be taught to seek happiness, he can be taught to just be happy. All he has to do is change his perception of what is success. Happiness lies not in who you are or what you have but rather in how you think.

Narcissism and capitalism are like husband and wife. Wherein one is the other is sure to be near. The narcissist is a product of capitalism. He grows up in a capitalist haze and is forever leeching off the system. In order for one to survive the intense heat of the capitalist doctrine, one assumes this narcissistic façade. Consequently everything becomes about image to the narcissist. He thrives in a world wherein he projects an astounding image to society. He lives and breathes to uphold a pristine projection. But he only adopts this approach because he occupies an insecure world. It is a defence mechanism designed solely for the injured party to live in this toxic capitalist environment. Thus the sufferer condemns himself to chains and lives a fraught tense existence of addiction. However this disease can be eradicated. If the narcissist can understand their motivations for living, they can begin to change them. But they first must see before they can rectify.

We desire to be successful not because of success but because of what it affords us. We want to feel wanted and being successful makes us feel wanted and liked. This is why we are engaged in a daily war with the system to be profitable. This is why we expend so much emotion in chasing success. However in the hunt of success, it becomes an addiction. We gain ground in some way but the effect dissipates and the addiction needs to be serviced in order to get the same high as before. This capitalist success (addictive happiness) is an artefact of materialism. It instils a belief in the individual that the world is a giant laboratory wherein to live or experience life one must accomplish. There are two types of success: One wherein one must cyclically succeed every day in order to be happy and one in which the individual feels successful for just existing. One is a capitalist success whilst the other is an Existential or Buddhist success. Success if anything is being who you are in a world that wants you to be someone else. We are prisoners of existence and as such we spend our days gazing out the steel windows at freedom, yearning for it, when all we have to do is be free and the concrete walls that enslave us will tumble. Look around you my friends. The world is the prison of which your perception retains the key.

Man wastes his life in search of a better one. He misuses the better years of his existence in a struggle to make himself more desirable to his peers. We live to make ourselves more covetable and desist on the pure desire to live. We want to be wanted and the drive is unconscious. We grow up and learn to feel good when we are in demand. Our existence becomes an inclination of desirability. This is narcissism. Being desired enables us to feel calm. Man is weak. He is a slave to being anticipated upon. It casts a shadow over his existence 24/7. Desirability is an addiction in that the feeling that accompanies one being desirable makes one feel good and the individual thus is consumed to hunger for this feeling repetitively. But failure is destined to occur. What happens when we grow old and lose our looks? What happens if the business fails? What happens if we get ill? One must grow up and see that all they need to be happy is themselves. They don't need to be coveted. It is a benefit if one is in demand, but one's life need not revolve around it. All one needs in this world to survive is food and a positive attitude. Don't be held ransom by the opinions of others. Don't be held in the psychological guillotine of desirability.

It is no coincidence that a relationship just happens to have two people. Why not three people or four people? The reason it is two people is because it is convenient. Conformity is convenience. We unconsciously embrace the system because it is the best system to meet our desires. But it is neither right nor wrong but rather appropriate. Napoleon could get legions of soldiers to die for him. How did he do this? He would seduce his soldiers and manipulate them emotionally. Conformity does the same trick with the hordes of men and women that inhabit this planet. Through education they have been made vulnerable emotionally and this schism in their conscience means they will seek marriage and work. One is only educated because this is what makes puppets out of individuals.

It is the personality of capitalism to encourage its disciples to want more. Enough is never enough under capitalism. The cancer becomes a fixation of which one cannot do without. They feel good after accomplishing in life but eventually the feeling diminishes and then in order to relive the experience a new accomplishment is craved. The problem in life is not that we don't have enough but rather that we have too much and don't appreciate what we do have. People thus are in a state of addiction. They are no better than the drug addicts. They are narcissistic addicts. But the addiction to capitalism or the addiction to money or the addiction to another individual is considered by society to be a healthy addiction. The way to live is through the Buddhist method. Be grateful to be alive in this world. One's own existence is more than enough to get by in life.

We chase the labels that we ascertain will generate happiness within. But this happiness is at the behest of our peer's opinion. Part of the reason we want to be in relationships and working a professional job is not because we enjoy doing those things, but because when we are seen to be occupied with these things, we earn acclaim from our peers, most noticeably our friends and family. We fear being victimized or silently slandered by our own friends. We recoil in their judgments. Relationships in particular become commoditized. What I mean by this is that we use the label of being in a relationship to promote our own projection. We don't venture into the relationship because we enjoy it, but rather we do so because it portrays a respectable status to our peers. So when they observe us in a relationship they will bestow respect upon us. A relationship such as this is a commoditized union. The relationship itself is like a product in the supermarket shelves that one purchases to improve their image. Just as a man buys a fast car or a woman buys a nice dress, so they will look better. So a man dates a woman who he thinks will improve his status among his friends and a woman dates a man who is in demand because this man makes her look good amongst her peerage. The relationship becomes an object to make those involved look good because looking good in the eyes of others makes them feel good. Again this stems from systematic education when young, that implores us to reward ourselves emotionally when we earn respect from our peerage. If one was educated individually and not collectively, people would mature differently.

Each and every single soul on this planet must sell themselves in order to acquire in this world. We have come to regard prostitution as the trade of sexual services, but it can also apply to man's daily struggle to make ends meet. A relationship for instance involves invisible trade. The man offers the woman something and vice versa. They don't just enter into a trade-less union. There must be gain on either side of the equation for it to be functional. Usually the male provides money and security in return for the sexual aspect of the female. But there is an exchange in goods. It may not be cash but it is other forms of currency. In work for instance a person provides a provision of which they are paid appropriately. The textbook sexual service does the exact same thing: An amenity is provided in exchange for cash. But because we wish to feel justified in living we never call it prostitution. It is labelled work or life and we buy into this model in an attempt to reassure ourselves that we are living the esteemed life.

We believe what we want to be true and not necessarily what is true. In our desperation to be coveted we do desperate things. Economies thrive on man's willingness to be deemed desirable. Man goes forth into the professional world intent on making himself more attractive to members of the opposite sex and the same can be said in part for women. But in our reckless nature to be treasured we can often make foolish decisions. Our lives thus reek of despair because in search of desirability we forfeit our happiness. We are involved in a never ending Darwinian chase of image. Our desperation brings wave after wave of stress upon us.

There are two groups of people in the world: The well-off 1% and the working 99%. The 99% slaves to make the 1% richer.

Most people desire to be in the 1%, but most are in the 99%. Most people will die forgotten and insignificant. They are fed lies by the 1%. They are told how virtuous working ones whole existence is and marriage is also extoled among other things. People are nothing and when you add up all the nothings you get something and that something is an economy. But the people want to be lectured on how worthy they are to society and the 1% give to the masses the illusion that they are laudable. But they are deceived. They will wake up in the twilight of their years wondering where it all went and only then will they realize that they were manipulated through education and propaganda to live a certain way.

Man grows up acclimatized to the capitalist mantra that he must take from the world to live. He wakes up every morning and says to himself that he must achieve today to be of worth. He becomes an addict to existence itself. Life becomes his drug of choice. But when he doesn't gain from the world he falls into a state of anxiety. Man would be wise to take guidance from the poorest people on earth for they appreciate life much more. The poorest of the poor must fight just to live. Every day becomes a battle and because of this they express much more gratitude to their cause than the man who has everything. The capitalist is under the illusion that life is perpetual. He approaches each day as if he is immortal. Thus he grows old and dies without ever having lived. Every day is a war against anxiety. He fears the opinions of his peers and this urges him to comply.

The better the standard of an economy, the more the people of that economy demand. The higher the quality of life of a social class, the higher their expectations for life are. Understandably this means that people will live a grand life, but it also means that they will put extreme pressure on themselves to meet the criteria of capitalism. This is the result of narcissism. Capitalism is a compulsion that never ends. The person like a fanatic achieves in some way or form and feels glowing. But after a period, the feeling dissipates and the individual must go back out into the landscape and try and achieve again. It mirrors addiction. The life of the shrewd capitalist is a never ending cycle of expectation. They must succeed to feel good and to feel good they must succeed. The happiest people in the world come from the poorest parts of the world because this cycle of obsession is not present. They are not under this invisible duress to succeed and to conciliate the herd. Instead of chasing financial success they must contend with hunger. Instead of chasing relationships they worry about shelter. They possess no herd or labelling anxiety. Their sole purpose is to try and survive in this frenetic universe.

We grow up believing that we have something great to announce to society. We grow up in a distinguished cloud of confidence wherein we expect to make our mark on life. But we all invariably end up living quiet lives of desperation. We offer nothing to this universe that it hasn't already seen and this realization is too daunting for some. For some they want to be remembered. They want to live a life less ordinary. But most succumb to the nothingness of life. This repetition is the silent adjudicator of our souls. We fail to see that we are living fruitless lives of repetition and that our wants and dreams are the same as everyone else's. People only see what they see when they wake up in the morning. They cannot see the awe inspiring universe. They cannot see the darkness that abounds them. They cannot prey on the universe for they do not acknowledge it. Perhaps if they did they would prize their existence a lot more. Perhaps if they could see, they would start to enjoy the sensation of being alive.

We live in a world that is infinite shades of grey. Nothing is ever black and white. Yet this is what so many do. They treat existence as black and white. They must be married to be of worth. They must have a solid career to be of esteem. They treat these different elements as single currency labels that they believe will procure happiness for them. They are guilty of being extremely narrow minded. Marriage may yield happiness but then again it may not and this is the gamble a person must take in life. This too applies to a career. We immigrate into college with dreams of this utopian life we will live but when we live it, it turns out to be different. We believe our happiness to be black and white. We are of the belief that doing certain things will yield happiness. But happiness does not work like that. One cannot decide to be happy but rather they simply become happy through living. But it is a game of uncertainty. One gets told by society that doing A, B and C will make him or her happy but it is not guaranteed. The surest way to be happy in the future is to be happy now. Just be happy to exist in this world despite its failures.

There is no right or wrong in life and yet we are damned to follow certain cliques in life. We believe categorically that our happiness lies in conforming. We take a chance. We say to ourselves: "My marriage will make me happy; my family will make me happy; my job will make me happy." We in effect attest to ourselves that if only we had this other more alluring life, everything would fall into place. This is a product of the capitalist narcissistic dilemma that infects so many in the western world. They remark that the grass is always greener in the other field, but life doesn't work like that. If you are not happy now, you can bet that you won't be happy in the future even if you manage to acquire the "dream life." This is because your whole mentality is carcinogenic; it is narcissistic. In order to become happy, you think you must change your life, when in fact you must change your perspective on life. It is your perspective that is tarnished not the way you live and you will continue to live a tormented existence as long as your viewpoint is diseased.

We chase in life and life cannot be chased. We chase the illusive happiness because we expect it to make us happy. We seek our dreams on the promise that when they are realized we will become content. It never works out that way. To truly enjoy life one must become grateful in the present. They must live in the moment and not be placing their hope on future expectations. Too many people hunt this grandiose sense of existence. They hunger to feel alive when existence is all they need. Chasing happiness wont yield happiness. Happiness by default cannot be obtained. But rather one must simply immerse themselves in life and hope that in doing so that they chance upon happiness. Of course just being excited to be alive is the most simplest form of happiness and yet the masses are not content to just be. They want life to give to them much more than it already gives. They don't realize that through simply being alive, life gives so much.

Addictive Happiness is a drug fuelled happiness that provides pockets of happiness to the individual but it never lasts. It is almost like a capitalist happiness that requires constant servicing in order to be maintained. If we succeed in some element of life we feel good. The mind then remembers this feeling unconsciously and seeks to sense it again. This gives birth to the addictive happiness of which I discuss. It is a powerful opiate but at the same time a deadly one for it sows the seeds of addictive behaviour. People become unconsciously directed to doing things in life that rebirth the sensation of feeling happy. Thus life becomes a Darwinian game of chase wherein we hunt out success not because it makes the world better or because it improves people's lives but because the successful person feels happy and this feeling is warm and comforting. It is however a plague. The happiness to aspire to is pure happiness. Pure happiness is not subordinate to success to be realized. This is the kind of elation that one experiences just for being able to exist on this planet. Whether you fail or succeed, whether it is raining or sunny, one feels not so much happy, but feels a rather sombre feeling of warmness due to the acknowledgement that they are alive and breathing in this universe. It is a Buddhist sense of realization that the world and existing in it, is your greatest achievement. The person then forgoes the addictive chase to be happy and settles for just being happy to be alive.

One must learn to find their own freedom in life. We get taught everything in life except how to teach ourselves. We get told how to live, how to be happy and how to die. Very few people thus live their own lives. They are living the lives of others. They are living according to how they should live them. The curiosity of going their own way, their own path has never been ignited. I think we get taught too much in life by the schools and colleges and thus the ability or the want to teach ourselves diminishes. We are prepared to accept what others say and do and as such we adopt this methodology as our own. We each have a voice but settle for the murmurings of the crowd.

If you know yourself and you know the world, you may never fear the rising sun. People are caught in a psychological bind. The world says do this and they oblige. But they find that what the world wishes of them produces much anguish. They are caught in quick sand. If they don't do what the world says they feel inferior; if they do what the world says they find that they come under stress. There exists a tragic disparity between what man wants to do and what he can do. Finding yourself thus should be the one thing that man aspires to. Find what you can do and accept what you cannot do. That is the secret to happiness.

Buddhism teaches us to let go of the materialistic race and become purveyors of our own happiness, our own freedom. Happiness can be found within. Man does not have to venture out into the dark recesses of the world to get high. He can if he is both brave and smart enough, find happiness within himself. Buddhism teaches among other things that man should become more tolerant of his boredom. This drive to avoid boredom is often the focal point of our problems. From the urge to avoid boredom stems the want to meet people and enjoy their company. But people by default are unpredictable. Thus the very people we depend on for our nourishment are often the same people who plague our existence with storms. The Buddhist stream of thought encourages man to find his inner soul and almost neglect his dependence on people for his happiness. If one wishes to be happy, just be happy to be alive.

One must view life as if they are very lucky to exist. The capitalist race has dissolved that thought within us. People wake up every day with one purpose: To accomplish in this world and through the uncertainty of accomplishment they feel a profound sense of calm. But the feeling dissipates in tandem with the sinking sun and the next morning they must triumph again in order to feel self-worth. One's existential freedom is obtained through realizing each and every day, that one is so lucky to be alive in this universe. Forget about the people and the cities, the traffic and the blue skies. Think of the planet revolving around the sun, think of the galaxies drifting through space. Think about how fortunate you are to be alive in this great world. When you become grateful for being alive you will become existentially free.

One needs to be more cynical in life to truly appreciate it. They must overcome their inherent narcissism. The nihilistic cynic is derided only because he sees the truth where others see normality. People are drugged. They see what they want to see. Life becomes about love and relationships when a great universe expands above our heads. Day to day activity becomes about jobs and careers, when ones mortality is only a breath away. The cynic fails to function in society because he does not buy into the life of conformity. He refuses to barter his life on ideals that will not yield happiness. Instead he tries to enjoy every second of his existence.

Religion is a means to keep the demons quiet. When man becomes self-aware he peers into the black hole of existence and what he sees frightens him. Where life once had meaning, now it is meaningless. Ones annihilation beckons in this universe. How does one deal with these two realities? One method is to fall into the arms of the divine. Religion preaches that man is not rudderless and this comforts him. It schools its followers on eternal life and this keeps the beasts of nihilism in hibernation. One must understand though, that god is a direct product of man and man is not a product of god. Without humans and without our ability to use language to dream, there can be no such thing as god. Alas when man finally dies, so too will his god.

We are moral because we are afraid. Man does not uphold the law because he deems the law to be right. He keeps within the constraints of the law because he fears the negative opinion associated with being criminal. This is also why man heeds to the will of conformity. He regards conforming as a means to limit a negative projection of him to the world. Men conform so that they can earn the respect of the herd. That a man has a wife and a career means his peers will attribute greater respect to him. That a woman has a husband and a family too means that she will inherit a greater respect from her community. We are afraid of our friends. It is the very people we love that we actually fear. The Will to Conform is violence masquerading as love. If we fall out with someone we despise we think nothing of it. If our friends and family become disgusted with our behaviour, we feel damned. Thus we live in their shadow at all times.

Through language we have created illusions. One of these illusions is true love. Does love exist or is it a placebo of our conscience. I am inclined to believe that love is just a model we have adopted that gives meaning to our existence. I think also that people are under pressure to find love in their life, so much that they remain unhappy until they can attest that they are finally in love. There is however no such thing as true love or the other half. These are just romantic articles the mind has come to believe. First and foremost man must love his own existence to be happy. This is the existential love for himself that he possesses through inhabiting a vast indifferent universe that rarely allows life to flourish. The problem is that through evolution and education both men and women have had it engrained in their heads that in order to be of virtue and worth, they must be in relationships. Consequently they believe that no other existence is acceptable. Furthermore they spend many a day unhappy with whom they are because they have failed to meet the criteria of what is stipulated.

Concentrate on you. Forget trying to make others happy to make yourself happy. Negate the greater world of which you are accustomed to. Think of the universe expanding and erupting in your mind. We are conditioned on the two dimensional aspects of life. The sunlight actually blocks out the realities of this world from us and it is only in the darkness that we can see the stars. People thus forget that they are animals. They forget that they inhabit a planet that revolves around the sun and that the sun is part of millions of stars that make up our galaxy. The universe can save you if you allow it to. The bleakness of nature can set you free. Release yourself into the world and never worry about another day in your life. Be happy because you can be happy. It is that simple.

Man must be awoken to the universe. It is not enough to wake up every day and see the sunrise. We have become too habituated on this ritual. Life becomes about the day to day suffering to appease the demands of conformity. As such the reality of this world is lost on us. Seldom do people realize that a great universe lies above and below them. Man despite his intelligence is still blind. The darkness of this world is stagnated by the blue skies. Life becomes about labouring. Relationships and work are encouraged and man's freedom is suppressed. Freedom if anything involves igniting ones consciousness to realize the truths of this world. Life is nothing. The planets and the galaxies will keep on turning with or without man. But one can find their consolation in this nihilistic opinion of the world. If one tears down the walls of conformity and finally sees the dark despairing universe for what it is, they may just become so grateful for being alive. In doing this they finally become happy because they realize how meaningless all their worries are and how lucky they are to exist in this universe. Don't think about jobs and relationships. Think in terms of how fortunate one is to exist in this world. When you do that, you negate your anxieties and become happy because you become appreciative of what you possess, which is a life and no matter how painful, a life is better than no life at all. Through being grateful, one finds their existential freedom.

There is no correct path on which to navigate through life. Life consists of many paths all of which are deemed correct and wrong. The goal of existentialism is to encourage the individual to find his own path be it based on the tapestry of conformity or not. That is all that is required of man. That he finds his own freedom in life and is not afraid to follow his heart. "No man ever followed his genius till it misled him," said Henry David Thoreau. One must follow their soul and not what is considered by the masses the correct path to pursue. Too many people think with their heads and not with their hearts. They look to the future and see themselves living this utopian life of grandeur. Consequently they do not listen to the murmurings of their soul. They ignore their true calling in favour of the popular choice. All one must do in life is find what they love doing. If you do what you enjoy you will love your existence. That is the ultimate goal of existentialism: To love your existence because you are so fortunate to exist in the first place. Being happy is the ultimate wealth, the only wealth. Conquer yourself above all else.

The End.

Essay Two

Part 1.1

Language is the light of civilization. It is the core reason why we experience the world as we do. Without it we would still be climbing the trees. But for what language gives us, it also takes away. With the weapon of language combined with eyesight, we can label - which means we can laugh, humiliate and degrade others. This haunts the individual to the pit of their conscience. The thought of being made fun of stirs something inside of them, a will to conform, because they understand all too well that conformity negates the power of stigma. Thus, to put two and two together, language leads to conformity and without it, conformity would not exist.

That we conform we hunger to find meaning in our existence. And through finding meaning we can become addicts, solely because we wish to experience anything other than boredom. In the 21st century that addiction is consumerism. Consumerism is the drug that sedates us, that keeps us content. It is a drug that is more powerful than an opiate. Consumerism in this day and age is not just buying more and more things we don't need; it is also our presentation to society, it is the job we work, it is the person we marry and so much more. We attempt to accrue all these things to look good in front of our peers. They control us, as do we them. Our lives become commoditized in a sense. Everything is treated as a commodity including our happiness, which is why it must be the same as everyone else's version of happiness. In essence we have become addicts - addicted to approval in every facet of our existence and it makes us mad and sad.

Part 2.1

To be known is regulation. This is why we are programmed to conform. Being seen by others adjusts our thought process. This is why there are so many narcissists, both male and female, because they are trying to determine how they are labelled by society. So men must be having sex with lots of women and women must be physically attractive - both then assume that they are liked because of it, that they have attained approval. This is the power of labelling within society. By simply being seen one is motivated by procuring approval. It dominates both adults and children, black and white, heterosexual and homosexual - when we are visually recognised, we desire to be liked than be disliked or ignored. When we are seen, a phenomenon I call the Labelling Anxiety takes place. Being seen produces a momentarily anxiety within our minds to which we respond by behaving in such a manner that we will be approved by those that see us. This includes those that dont know us personally as much as those that do. Thus we become image conscious beings who need to be showered in "likes" in order to function. And it is this very obsession with approval that makes us suffer and be miserable.

The female at all times wishes to receive positive approval from the male and the male vice versa from the female. Labelling truly goes a long way to determining societies of today. But why the obsession? The answer is that being approved by others makes us in turn feel so good about ourselves. Approval is akin to a drug like cocaine or heroin. It turns us on. It makes us feel content. That is why we are consumed by it. And we learned to live such a way in childhood, through parenting, education and urbanization. Those three things train us to seek out positive approval in order to be gratified. The narcissist only takes these things to the extreme, in that they need approval from the whole world, something which is not feasible. Ultimately what I am suggesting is that labelling can be applied to everyone and not just the criminals of society. Sociology only applies labelling theory to the deviant, when in reality it governs all in society on the whole.

But what happens when we are not approved, as in rejected or demeaned? That we are so conditioned on the system we become melancholic. For example the young male that wants females to like him, but is rejected by most, becomes full of hatred of women and may become violent. But violence is just the end, of which labelling was the start. He wants women to positively label him at all times. He wants attention. He wants adoration. When he does not get it, he becomes disconsolate and vengeful. But it all started in the group setting, either in the home, the classroom or the neigbourhood. Perhaps if he grew up all alone on an island by himself would he only truly be happy and mature. But there is no Starbucks or McDonalds on this island. This indicates the dilemma faced by both men and women within the system. If they are part of the system, they must be status conscious. That is the price they pay for being in the system. But if they try to avoid it all by living alone, they more than likely won't have much money to buy the commodities needed to survive.

But this labelling mechanism (which I call The Labelling Phenomenon in my other notes) truly dominates day to day life. When one is walking up a busy city street for instance, they are labelling everyone they see, despite not personally knowing them. And they in return are labelling us. Thus the individual instinctively learns to become conscious of how he or she is labelled, even by those they don't know. It is blind its operation and few are cognizant of what they are doing and why they are actually doing it. One does not observe the mechanism, only its result.

Look at the stigmatization of the eccentric. He is labelled odd or weird. Or look at how the sexual virgin is demeaned, or the homosexual or the sexual deviant. We dont want to be associated with such labels and as such we behave in such a way to avoid them. This is a huge component of why we obsess over marriage and working a job of prestige - both those things lead to us being positively labelled by society. It takes the stigmatization of the eccentric to produce conformity in the rest of us. One could make a case that it takes crime and mental illness for society to flourish because the average individual is so disgusted at the thought of being associated with the criminals or the severely mentally ill. Work backwards from the criminals and the escorts and the latent homosexuals. They fear being reported on. They fear being known. They know they will not be approved. Now analyse mainstream society. They have no anxiety or trepidation in exposing their identity to the herd. But society is still there, analysing ruthlessly. Thus, they instead live for society's approval and endorsement. When you expose your full identity to society, seeking approval becomes a by-product. Few realize this and even fewer can defy it.

We are guilty of tying our happiness to image in the capitalist system. When we look good we in turn feel good about ourselves. So a man tries to climb the corporate ladder to such a position where he earns millions in bonuses and a woman looks for a certain man to marry, one that makes other women jealous. We are really motivated by procuring approval unlike anything else. The herd ultimately controls us, no matter how much we deny it. But the worrying thing is what happens when our image takes a hit? What happens to the man who loses his high-income job? How does he feel then? Or what happens if the man who the woman holds in high regard commits a crime? How does she feel then? You are in some ways playing with dice when depending on image to be the cornerstone of your happiness, because a good image can vanish very quickly.

The modern-day man and women are under enormous pressure to be the modern day man and woman. They must follow their gender controls. A man must be the perfect husband, father, friend, son and employee. The woman must be the perfect wife, mother, friend, daughter and employee. If they are healthy psychology wise they call this living, when really it is an imprisonment. But of course the best prison is always the one where the prisoners don't realize they are imprisoned. What keeps them going? What keeps them obedient? Simple really, it is consumerism. They are prepared to make others rich at the expense of themselves, so long as they have enough money to buy things they don't really need. This sedates them and the things they own end up owning them.

The law-abiding individual must fear interpretation where the criminal counterpart only fears the bullets of a gun. We are, to be honest, petrified of being known, although we don't recognise this or accept it. But when we walk into the office where we work, we fear what our work colleagues think of us and as I have suggested this is a chief reason why we conform - to neutralize this social fear. We are not free for social reasons as much as financial or effort ones. By saying hello to those we know, that is precisely our punishment for existing in the community. The person that keeps to himself and avoids the community gets ostracized, something which gives the common man nightmares. Of course it could be much worse - we could be famous and then have millions of people judging us and cancelling us and so forth. But it cannot be underestimated, one is living in a prison in the community. You cannot see it but it is a prison system, with its own rules and punishments for those that defy it. It could be compared to a cult, where a small few at the top benefit from the delusion at the bottom. And it only functions because of happiness. You condition people on how they can become happy and then you give them just about enough money to be able to attain that happiness.

The power of labelling controls us. Women suggest that "real men don't hire sex workers." How does this affect men? It funnels them into marriage as the means to acquire sex. If they procure sex from anything outside of a relationship, they get labelled a sex pest or creep. But men are returning serve on the female - if the woman is having too much casual sex, she is the labelled a slut by the male. Both sexes thus control each other for the economic systems gain. They are forced to be good law-abiding citizens by each other. Thus a positive label does not exist in this world. A positive label is just a means of control like a negative one is. In order for a husband to continue to be positively labelled by his wife, he must fulfil obligations, as must the wife to continue to be liked by her husband.

I remember reading about a man who was on disability for his bad hearing. He said that his mother, although not narcissistic, was putting him under pressure to get a job and have friends. Now analyse why she was doing this. She was doing it because she wanted her son to fall under the correct labels. In other words, she was afraid of how he was interpreted. She associated those who did not work and who had no friends, as being eccentric delinquents. When people asked her, what was her son doing, she was embarrassed by having to tell these people that he was doing nothing. Again, she was governed by labels and she was not even a full-blown narcissist. "Stigma is a process whereby the reaction of others spoils normal identity." - Erving Goffman.

Desire and labelling thus come into conflict quite often. A man desires sex but has to be careful how he attains it for he could be negatively labelled as an outcome. Then we desire to earn money, if not are forced to, but must deal with the bureaucracy of those that we work with. Freud suggested we are repressed which is most true. There are so many things we wish we could do, but we understand we will be negatively labelled should we appease our desires. Thus as Thoreau suggested "we live quiet lives of desperation." It is possibly the best quote I have read about how one is shackled by the system and society in general.

Labelling it must be said only applies to humans. No other animal is afraid of being laughed at by another animal. A cat may fear a dog physically but not mentally - as it is not afraid of being mocked by the dog. Humans on the other hand must fear other humans psychologically. Laughter is a most terrible weapon, an equivalent of the atom bomb in psychiatric terms. It destroys the mind of the unfortunate individual. Either they develop serious psychiatric illness or they become narcissistic and vengeful. The whole male incel problem in western societies can be traced back to laughter - such a young man asks out a girl in his class or neighbourhood and she turns him down, laughing that she would never ever date such a guy like him. This causes the young man to become extremely resentful and it just builds and builds until he shoots dead a few people. Now I am not blaming the woman - she is entitled to choose who she chooses. What I am trying to convey is just exactly what laughter does to our minds. Labelling is an assault, a psychological one, just as if we were physically assaulted. It hurts us in its own way.

Suicide as well is a question of labelling - not in every suicide but in so many. So many commit suicide because they are not positively labelled. Or perhaps they were positively labelled but lost such a label to be negatively labelled. Perhaps they cannot get a job, which means they are being negatively labelled by potential employers during the interview stage. Or else (which is more common) they cannot get a partner. They go on date after date and are rejected. And being rejected for the extremely insecure individual is akin to losing a limb. But all this is, is the power of a label among individuals. The insecure of society are so addicted to being labelled appropriately that it confines them to immaturity. Their whole journey of existence becomes one of labelling gratification and not one of sincere enjoyment. They marry, they work, they conduct themselves all so they can be positively labelled by their peerage. To escape this wrath of labelling is to mature.

Labelling also distracts us from reality. Earth is not reality. It is an anomaly. You won't find it anywhere else in the universe. Reality is darkness; it is bleakness; it is nothing. That is the universe. Yet most people living day to day are not cognizant of this. Why? I feel they are distracted by maintaining their interpersonal relations with others. Being positively labelled matters more, understandably, than the universe. As one is walking up a busy shopping centre, you are not thinking of the universe, but instead you are thinking of how these other people interpret you. You are distracted by the labelling anxiety. Ultimately our exposure to the herd regulates us.

It is interesting in that in using an anonymous identity on some internet forum, we behave differently than that of the real world where people know our full identity. This is what I am attempting to impart to you - once known you adjust your behaviour to be positively labelled by those you know. On the anonymous forum you are more likely to be condescending and rude. You, if you are mature, don't behave like this when talking to your work colleagues or neighbours. Thus if one truly wishes to live life on their terms, limiting how many people know you would be a good place to start. But for the working middle class, this is not feasible.

Labelling has soiled love as well in that we often select our partner based on if others would select him or her too. This especially applies to the female of society who is choosing a man that other women want. If more women want him and would be jealous, then the woman in question will select the said man. Labelling, as in the reward of a positive label, has such an influence in what we choose. If it makes us look good relative to our peers, we will choose it or buy it. We are always unconsciously saying to ourselves: If I am seen with this (be it a person or a house or a piece of clothing), how will the herd interpret me? Your mind is frequently asking this question. What it conveys is that ultimately you are afraid of what people think of you and as such try to engineer your projection in such a way that you are validated.

The pressures of being known and labelled are intense. Numerous people have commit suicide over being labelled, some even because they were positively labelled. Ross Lockridge Jr who was a writer commit suicide weeks after the publication of his famous book "Raintree County." "I walk past people and I wonder what they think," he said in his despair. Truman Capote also expressed similar tones after his book In Cold Blood, which made him famous and he suggested that it killed him. I guess one must understand that more tears are shed over answered prayers than unanswered ones. Then there are numerous examples of people who have won the lotto and regretted it, saying that it turned their closest against them. The pressures of labelling can also be understood by our direction towards social appearance. Why do most women have long hair? Why do most men have short hair? Well the power of labelling answers these two questions, in that we don't wish to be negatively labelled by choosing to deviate from societal standards. Imagine the horror of being famous, being known by every single person in your city or country. It is not a good proposition. And one would only value their anonymity in such a situation.

Now there is no solution to this dilemma of labelling unless we live all alone in a shed in the woods. We are born to parents, we are forcibly educated and we live in the community, three things that enforce labelling upon us. The best you can do is try to limit how many people know you. Have your parents and siblings, have three good friends in the community and two good work colleagues. And then try to limit meeting others.

It is through labelling that an equilibrium in society is achieved. You can see this equilibrium when walking down a busy city street. Everyone tries to avoid bumping into everyone else. We keep to ourselves. We dont do anything out of the ordinary like start shouting. But the equilibrium is disturbed if someone acts eccentrically. For example if someone took off all their clothes, that situation would be labelled negatively. So as I suggest, labelling stabilizes society. The threat of being negatively labelled (stigmatized) dictates how we behave in the real world. Thus stigma is vital for societies to function if not to prosper.

Labelling produces a sort of bind within people. Because of the threat of a negative label, we do things we don't wish to do. For example, imagine if a colleague at work asks you out for a few drinks after work. You initially decline. Then the next week he or she asks again. You decline again. Then the week after he or she asks again. Now you are afraid to decline over the fear of him or her falling out with you. Thus you go out for drinks after work this third time of asking, purely so he or she who asked you, won't dislike you. This is the labelling bind brought on by the labelling anxiety. Social media is a prime example of the Labelling Bind. If we choose not to be on social media, we get negatively labelled and thus this threat motivates us to be on social media to avoid a negative label. The Labelling Anxiety makes us fear being labelled negatively, so we go on social media to be part of the crowd (The Labelling Bind).

"We are all just actors trying to control and manage our public image, we act based on how others might see us." - Erving Goffman. We behave in a way that enables us to be positively labelled. To add to this, we then pretend to be happy because this is how the system tells us to be happy. The insecure (and often narcissistic) individual then says: "I look happy; therefore, I must be happy." This is Pretence Happiness. But is one actually happy?

Because of labelling you are locked in "I need" mode. You need a good job, a good partner, a good car, a good house, a good set of clothes, good gadgets. You need all these things because you want people to be impressed by you. Ergo you are dependent on people to like you in order to like yourself. This is the height of immaturity, to need external validation in order to feel good internally, driven by society's stranglehold over you. Honestly, validation must come from within - and that is the difference between those that are grateful and those that are not.

Seldom does one blame society for their woes. It is the government or the economic system or the boss or others in general. One just cannot see how society impedes them. They are so normalized on society that it is not society's fault in their mind. Interaction with others is in my opinion the chief reason for ones problems in life. But people still invite others into their existence, only adding to the conundrum. That we still get anxious in the system despite the advancements in general is the most damning indictment of society.

One can think of the maze of being known through analysing some famous criminal such as Pablo Escobar. That he was so known was the reason he acquired his wealth, but also his downfall. He was the most wanted terrorist at the time of his death. He was chased and hounded all over Colombia. Was it worth it in the end? It's a rhetorical question really. But that is the problem with being too known in society. You eventually get cancelled.

Part 3.1

The state is in control. The state is determining how you think. It is through the institution of education that one is manipulated to think and hence behave a certain way. Not alone are the teachers teaching us, but all the students are teaching each other also - how to behave, what to wear, what to think, what to accept and what to reject. It is because of the children teaching the children that the child matures into an adult that is materialistic and herd driven. They learn in the classroom to appease their peerage before themselves. When others like them, they in turn like themselves. They then carry this mentality in adulthood and sadly few grow out of it. Thus one to mature must always question what they are taught and not just casually accept it.

So how does this young individual attain endorsement from their fellow classmates? Simple, they must conform to the group's ideology. The must want what others want and hate what others hate. Education is indoctrination. It even rhymes with it. It is the most effective method of the state controlling its citizens for the benefit of the state. Of course, the brainwashing is so effective that few realize they are conditioned. They are brainwashed to believe they are in fact not brainwashed. They become addicted to the currency of happiness in order to be fulfilled and thus spend the remainder of their lives in a futile hunt to become happy - something they never achieve.

Through urbanization and education, we get introduced to the herd and thus condemned forever, unless we are a rare individual that possesses the courage to defy the herd and go their own way. But most lack such a conviction. They are so afraid, terrified of being shunned by those that know them, that they interact with the community for the duration of their lives. They would if it came to it, rather lose the love of their partner than that of the community, such is the hold that the community has over them. And who truly gains from this regulation by the community? It is not the community itself. No, they are just taken advantage of. Who truly gains in this cult is the people at the top, ergo the state. I suppose the tragedy of it all is that we never question our education and enrolment within the community. We just accept the path laid out for us.

I cannot emphasize it enough: the reason you automatically think of the family unit as the means to be content is because of society. It is a product of your conditioning by the community - from school all the way up to college graduation. The equation is simple: when you are around people you tend to be regulated. Being around people manipulates you into wanting certain things just so you will be approved by those who interact with you. You don't wish to be thought of as mentally ill or homosexual or even a deviant - thus you acquire the family unit for stigma reasons.

Look at what they are teaching in the schools. They don't lecture you on the absurdness of life. They don't teach you about how worthless life truly is. They teach you things that encourage you to conform, to work all your life to make money for someone else, to acquire the family unit to be respected, to pay your taxes to a government that takes from you. They don't even teach psychology in schools because they don't want you to understand yourself, because that is most dangerous. They want you to live on your instinct - and what is your instinct? It is to conform.

Education has the same effect as social media. On social media one lives for likes. The same happens to the child in the classroom. They live for approval from other children. When people like them, they like themselves. Education does the same thing to us as children, in that we instinctively learn that happiness is making our classmates be impressed by us. Then we just carry this narcissistic attitude into adulthood and conformity is in part a by-product of this. Ok, it is not all bad. The collectivised education of children does produce a compassionate society. But a huge negative is insecurity. What education does is make us think that we need others in our lives. It makes us numb to the threats that others carry. We cannot see that once known by others we become encaged by their opinion of us. The reality is that to be mature one must possess the courage to be disliked, especially by their community. But most would rather be taken advantage of than be disliked.

To become mature is not to reject your education but to add to it. You enhance it by educating yourself, by questioning things, by being curious as to why they are educating you in the first place. One must in theory take what the standard education gives them and reach a point where they start to educate themselves. As Mark Twain said: "You should never let school interfere with your education." Alas most lack either the intelligence or maturity or both to do this. Thus they become puppets for the state and remain so all their life.

Part 3.2

Education, urbanization and parenthood lead to being known and being known leads automatically to conformity. Conformity is a direct response to being labelled. One such problem is that people become so afraid of being different for standing up to conformity that they are forced to conform as if a loaded gun is pressed against their forehead. It is those that deviate from the trappings of conformity that generally get mislabelled and this fear strikes into the heart of the weak individual, who then conforms. The reality is that the state pushes one to conform and stigmatizes those that don't, because conformity benefits the state. What is legit in life is only so because the economic system benefits. What is considered incorrect is only so because it hurts the economic system.

A flaw with conformity is that our lives are built around it to such an extent that we cannot see the true reality of the universe. Who recognizes the universe as they drive to work? Who is cognizant that they are composed of trillions of atoms as they deal with life's hardships and problems? Instead, we are knowledgeable about football teams and famous models. We are naive and dumb. This gives rise to what I term Economic Narcissism. What I mean by this is that our frame of reference is the economic system. It is not the universe. We are slaves to daily life under the economic system. We cannot see the stars and kidneys in our bodies - life becomes solely about earning enough money to buy more and more commodities.

The idiosyncrasy of the economic system can be best explained by the billions who devote themselves to a sports enterprise. This is the definition of foolishness. The fan cares about the sports team, but the sports team does not care about the fan. Yet billions of people worldwide are fanatical about supporting such and such sports teams. The sports player can make millions out of it. But what does the average fan get from supporting his or her team? If the team wins a match, the fan feels good for a couple of hours. That is all he or she stands to gain. The fact that so many are devoted followers of sports teams demonstrates just how easy it is for the economic system to condition people to behave in such a way that benefits the cult that is the economic system. Intelligent life from another galaxy would laugh at us and how easy we are to seduce. That we have all these addictions without realizing the true scope of the universe is insanity. But when one person is mad, he gets sectioned; when billions are mad, it is normality.

Conformity schools us on earning money to survive. But there is a contradiction with regards to this. We spend most of our time earning money that we sacrifice our health. Then when we get older and our health is declining rapidly, we take all our money earned and try to rectify our ill health. But by then it is too late for the damage is chronic.

The propaganda pertaining towards conformity is relentless. Films, books, music songs, parents, the community, politicians and so on, all suggest in different methods that the solution to your life is to work all your life so you can afford your family. The individual is drowned in so much propaganda that they have no frame of reference as to what else they can do with their lives. They are so brainwashed on conformity that everything else is a disease. A bird locked in a cage all its life thinks flying is an illness. Society is putting one under enormous pressure to conform, pressure that is invisible. No one can see it or feel it, but only react to it. This is the power of being labelled.

Cognitive Dissonance can in part explain the infatuation with conforming. The young individual is brainwashed that there is only one path to live and as such learns to live in the future at the expense of the present. "Once I am 30 and possess X, Y and Z, then I will be happy." They then reach 30 years old and are still unhappy. Then they say: "Once I am 40 years old, and have accumulated X, Y and Z, then I will be happy." Then they reach that age and are still unhappy, and you can see where I am going. The economic system makes people live in the future at the expense of the present. But it deceives them for the only thing waiting in the future is one's death.

Ultimately it is subtle fear that motivates us to conform. Imagine telling your parents you wish to remain single for most of your life? Or imagine telling your friends and co-workers the same thing? It will lead to a loss of respect within the community. It will lead to gossip and who can bear being negatively gossiped about? Very few, it must be said. Conformity has though become the means by which economies flourish. If you took a leaf out of George Orwell's book and forced everyone to marry and have children, they would more than likely rebel. But casually suggest that you won't become happy unless you conform and they become meek and desperate. In Western cultures it is Aldous Huxley's philosophy that is in operation. People are living in a prison in such places but because of consumerism they are sedated with happiness much like a heroin addict is on their drug, and this maintains law and order.

There are two types of conformity: Mature Conformity and Immature Conformity. Immature Conformity is desperation. Such a person is deeply anxious about missing out on happiness and life in general by not acquiring the dream life. The thought of going family less as you journey through existence drives them to depression. This is not healthy. One will more than likely put themselves into dysfunctional relationships because of their desperation. Mature Conformity in contrast one recognizes that they possess choice. They can conform and be happy. But they can also go against the current and be happy. Either way they are happy. This person is mature and lacks desperation. They are not narcissistic and are all in all the type of person that should get married, ironically.

One cannot doubt the power in the present age of social media in motivating the conformists. Just as the herd implores one to hit the targets, social media does the same if not amplifies this. Naive boys learn that they must be successful and rich; naive girls learn that they must be beautiful in order to be liked. This makes them melancholic if they fail to reach this threshold. The male incel culture and the radical female feminist, both who are deeply flawed, are spawned in youth either through the community or social media, but most likely both. And I would wager that these two types were rejected or are rejected by society and they become hostile and bitter because of it - the male incels blame women and the radical female feminists blame men. A predictable response when you don't wish to take responsibility for your life.

The alarming element of conformity is that one fully believes they are free. This could not be further from the truth. You are enslaved in a system that tricks you or conditions you to believe that you are free. And all those in actual prisons are the ones that are bondaged in some form. But if one is so free, why are so many people protesting? Why is the suicide rate so high? Again the illusion of consumerism tricks people into convincing themselves that they are free because they have money to buy things. Consumerism is the mind controlling drug of Western cultures. In truth we are living in our own prison, although we deny this. But two threats sedate or suppress our own internal mutiny: One, we fear being negatively labelled should we deviate from conformity if we even dare question it. Two, we are petrified of missing out on happiness by not conforming.

It is worth mentioning the different worries or anxieties that plague the modern man in contrast to our hunter gatherer relatives. The latter worried about food and shelter and warmth. The modern man has those three things in abundance but still worries. He worries about standing in the community and losing his job. Perhaps some time in the future man will have no worries. But I suspect you do not get a society in such a scenario.

What then are the young successful and rich entrepreneurs doing that the slave who must work till 70 isn't. Well one obvious thing they are doing is not conforming in their teens and early twenties and instead working hard in that time with their business and so forth. You see most teenagers are engaged in sexual selection, that is they are trying to be selected by the opposite sex. So the boys must be the best on the sports team and the girls must be physically attractive. But those that defy this and instead concentrate on their careers tend to succeed more than those that are obsessed with being sexually selected. On a personal note, the best student in my class when I was at school was the girl who just studied all the time instead of chasing boys. She is now a consultant in the medical discipline and probably won't ever have to worry about money in her life.

Part 3.3

Narcissism is a predictable reaction to the economic system. When faced with the onslaught of labelling, it is a natural response to try to be approved. The narcissist takes this approval to a whole new level. Everything they do is built around attaining "likes." Ultimately it consumes them and retains them in a state of childness. The narcissist has not matured - they are still in adolescence consumed with approval. He or she works, marries and lives to sustain an image to the viewing public, even though it is the nature of humankind to not really care about others. But the narcissist is convinced they do care. They suffer an intense Labelling Anxiety and live an inauthentic existence built around mass approval.

They then feign happiness. They pretend to be happy. They seek the gratification of applause and call that gratitude when it is the very opposite to gratitude. The narcissist can never be grateful, they are too immature to do so. They are also seldom with people in their lives, and this also only adds to their childish petulance. Driven by insane levels of competition they become envious of others who have accomplished more than them. Of course, the other two elements of the dark triad often occur as well: psychopathy and Machiavellianism. The consumerism of life is what motivates the narcissist - he or she wants to be seen or perceived as the very cream of society.

Narcissism is just the psychiatric term for deeply insecure people. One in ten are full blown narcissists. Think about that for a second. This equates to millions upon millions of narcissists. And how many are not full-blown narcissists, but display some narcissistic traits? Millions upon millions more. The esteemed life is a symptom of narcissism. The man that needs the beautiful woman and the big mansion and the fast cars, conveys narcissism in abundance. And such a man, despite his wealth, can never be happy. What would it take to make him happy? His answer is always "more." As the saying goes "Much wants more," and that is especially true of the standard narcissist.

The male narcissist believes himself to be doing something right as he is being selected by women, young women it must be said. But young women are anything but mature, who themselves are governed by image and money, and consequently find the male narcissist so attractive. But he can attract the female admirers, but he cannot keep them. They all eventually sever ties with him, not that he cares, as it is sex that interests him.

But the whole premise of narcissism is labelling. He or she likes themselves when others like them. They approve of themselves when others approve of them. Approval as already stated is a drug like no other, that consumes its victim, and makes them do desperate things. Validation for the narcissist is always external and not internal. And they will justify their behaviour when they see how many people follow them on social media or in the real world. But so long as the interact with others they cannot become mature. But the honest truth is that validation must always come from within and not others. Others can take back their approval at any time. What happens if the said narcissist loses his wealth or his looks or is arrested for some crime. Fundamentally it is a much better proposition to be happy without approval than be happy because of approval.

The capitalistic parasite infects so many of our youth nowadays. Its venom tells them that they need to be famous and wealthy in order to be happy. Surrounded by others (their peers) through education and urbanization, they learn that it feels much better to be loved than to be ridiculed. Thus, they become devoted servants of narcissism and only few can change themselves, and not without some form of guidance. I suppose the only positive is society, in that the standard narcissist will more than likely have a family. Whereas the really mature grateful individual, the opposite of the narcissist, is less likely statistically to have children.

The narcissist can be best summed up by the phrase that they Live-For-Others. They live for external adoration. Rather than live for oneself and be happy and find reward in being alive in the universe, the narcissist lives for image, unaware of the universe and the enormous luck that gave rise to them. That is the thing about narcissistic people, they fully believe they were destined to succeed, if they do in fact succeed. Whereas mature people recognise how important chance was or is in their fortune. But what if the narcissist does not succeed or sees others succeeding. Then the self-hatred kicks in. They become disgusted with themselves and resort to blaming others for their own sabotage.

Narcissism is one of the worst things about Western culture - a culture where it is as good as it is going to get in the present age to live, and yet there are so many toxic self-loathing and self-pitying individuals within the culture. You would think that the life they have and the freedom afforded, would make them grateful, but instead it makes them reptilian in nature. The mass murderers of America are unquestionably bitter narcissists that are just possessed by resentment and that they have failed and that it is society's fault for their failure.

Part 3.4

Despite the fact that we live in an age of wealth and advancement, there are still so many anxious and miserable people. What is happening? Well capitalism makes them insecure. Ironically prosperity has the opposite effect in that it leads to narcissism and immaturity. This is what I call The Capitalistic Insecurity. Such a person may have wealth and a high standard of living, and yet they feel a void in their lives, as though something were missing. Part of the problem is that we are always comparing ourselves to both others and this template that signifies what one needs in order to be happy. Thus, when we fail to hit the targets laid down by this template or when we see others succeeding, the mental anguish hits us hard. Such a person is childish and extremely naive - blind really to the universe and the chance of life on this planet.

The Capitalistic Insecurity manifests itself in so many ways. The sufferer needs to be rich, successful, attractive, popular, smart, living the good life and so on. When they do not hit these targets, they become melancholic. What they fail to grasp is that it is society that has made them feel like this - society has chosen their dreams and also their nightmares. The individual fails to realize that it is the people in their lives, their friends, family and work colleagues, that control the individual - that make them materialistic and vain. Such individuals are still children, locked in the adolescence phase of maturity, where they need to be liked in order to like themselves. That we see everyone else doing it, we become conditioned to want it ourselves.

A woman once asked: "I am unattractive - how do I deal with this?" The capitalist method is to pay a plastic surgeon 30,000 dollars to mutilate your face. The mature method is to stop trying to be liked in order to like yourself. Stop needing external approval from others in order to feel good about yourself. But most opt for the former because the drug of approval sedates like no other. But you can apply this to one's whole life in general. Everything they do is built around retrieving approval from those that know them. If only they could learn to be grateful and find peace within themselves and stop seeking validation like a heroin addict.

Eliot Rodgers was a man who had everything if you were looking from the outside in. He had money, was living in the dream country, was good looking etc. Why then did he kill six people and injure fourteen others? The answer is the Capitalistic Insecurity. Life had told him that in order to be of value, he had to have a beautiful woman by his side. He had to be working the esteemed career. If he was not doing these things, he was in the eyes of the American capitalistic culture, failing. It was not that he did not have enough. He had too much and did not appreciate what he had; he had too much and needed more.

Ironically, and this is amazing, that the happiest people live in the poorest countries and not the richest countries. Isn't that astonishing! With capitalism comes pressure and one also can lose everything. The more one has, the more one can lose, and when they do lose it drives many to suicide. Then the pressure is enormous in wealthy countries - you are pressure at your job where targets must be met and then pressure in the community, where you have to maintain strong bonds and solidarity with everyone else, or else you get ostracized. Whereas in contrast in poorer countries people just work on farms and grow their own food, at their own pace. There isn't as much stress and they don't stand to lose as much should things go bad. An interesting story is one about the North Korean man that escaped a concentration camp in North Korea and fled to South Korea. He made an interesting point that despite the terrible conditions in the concentration camp, no one commit suicide. Yet every day in Seoul, he heard of someone killing themselves. It makes you think.

Everyone when finished school should really go on welfare for a year and live on the bare minimum. Such a life would teach you to value what you have. It would teach you how to be grateful. They could learn to live without money, they could learn to live without food, they could learn to live with rejection and so on. In contrast the multimillionaire capitalist has so much that he wants more and lacks gratitude.

Part 4.1

A relationship is a natural response to being known and hence being labelled. That we become known, we adjust our presentation in such a way that we are approved. One such way to achieve this approval is through love. This is a huge reason why so many are obsessed with romance, not for the enjoyment they can get from being in a relationship itself, but for the recognition they receive when they are seen dating a person of prestige. If one thing has been corrupted by narcissism and the eagerness to be approved, it is love. Thus, it is most difficult to find a mature partner, given that so many want love for the incorrect reasons.

Love as well is the method of avoiding stigma and this is huge reason for its popularity. We want sex but understand that we can get in trouble if we attain it in a deviant manner. Men can be labelled sex pests and women can be slut shamed. Thus love suppresses this stigma. Love becomes the only means to engage in sex and not be negatively labelled by the herd. This is an enormous reason for its popularity, a reason most are oblivious to.

There then exists authentic love and inauthentic love. True love can be categorized as the latter. There is no one person you are supposed to find, that is perfect in every way, with flaws, that loves you unconditionally and only you. If you believe in true love, it signifies that you are immature and childish. What actually exists is authentic love and it is not this one thing you are supposed to find. It is also difficult to maintain - there will be troughs along the way, that will only serve to make the bond stronger. Ironically it is the individual that is not obsessed with love and that could live alone all their lives, that possesses the skills to thrive in a relationship. They are the most mature people. As such, the individual that yearns for love to complete them is always the most immature and naive individual.

Alas love is vital for the system, not just because it keeps the birth rate stable, but also because it drives men and women to make themselves attractive to potential mates, something that adds to the economic system. Women select the competent and confident man with resources. Men select the attractive woman. This is a huge part of the reason why there are fewer female geniuses than male ones, not because women are in some way inferior to men, but because sexual selection dominates most people's thoughts and as I suggest men are selecting the attractive female, not the smart or hardworking one.

If you analyse two people that have known each other since childhood and are mature and lack narcissism, their love is authentic. These are two people living for each other and not for the world. In contrast, think of the toxic early thirties person that is so motivated by the herd and to attain approval that they are desperate to be seen married, just so they can procure endorsement. This is a toxic relationship and probably won't stand the test of time. Is one in a relationship to make themselves happy or to make others happy? That is what one must ask themselves.

Having said that, marriage is forced upon men and women alike. They are under severe duress from friends and family and co-workers to achieve a certain level of status in their life. Of course, the state does not criminalize love as it does the sex industry, which is another force that guides people to marry and have children. All in all the herd decides so much of our choices. Free choice is an illusion. What you will become as you grow old has been decided since you were four years old.

I am not suggesting that the rich man and the attractive woman cannot find love. But they must be so careful and do their due diligence when choosing a partner. Both these people possess traits that the narcissistic of society admire. "Is this person dating me because they truly like me or because I make them look good?" That is what the rich man and the attractive woman must probe. Regardless of your gender, you must turn down the individual that is hyping you up to be something you are not. For what happens when they no longer put you on a pedestal? The relationship will disintegrate.

Having said all that, living alone is still the more secure form of existence. A relationship is akin to rolling dice in a casino -

it can all go wrong and very quickly at that. The melancholia then experienced when the relationship breaks up really hits hard. But what if we had never been in a relationship? What if we were content to just live alone and be grateful for the chance to exist? Wouldn't we be in a much better position?

Part 4.2

It is a world where being happy is the number one goal. That we are known means we try to best manage our presentation to society and our peers. We call this happiness. So we acquire the family unit, live in a nice house, buy all these commodities so we can show others that we are happy. But in reality we are miserable slaves. These things we own, end up owning us. Ironically the desire and quest to be happy actually prevents one from actually being happy. This is called the Paradox of Hedonism. You cannot become happy by wanting to be happy now or sometime in the future. All you can do in life is let the dice fall where they may and hope that you feel a sense of gratitude at some stage.

The more one yearns to live, the less they do. The more they try to enjoy life, the less they do. One cannot conjure happiness out of the thin air. As I suggest you must go through life and hope to experience happiness in the form of gratitude. The narcissistic in particular are corroded by being happy to show off to their peers. They always demand more. They get envious when someone has a better life than them. But as they think like this, they just push themselves deeper into the abyss.

The pursuit of happiness is linked to labelling because in pursuing and attaining happiness we suppress the Labelling Anxiety. This is why so many put happiness as their number one goal in life, for presentation management reasons. Living the good life prevents us from being stigmatized and ostracized by the community. Happiness is not a dream but a form of regulation.

The narcissist such is their ego and level of self-obsession demands an experience from life at all times. When they enter a shop to buy a bar of chocolate, they want an experience. When they have sex, they want an experience. When they watch a film, they want an experience. But this is precisely why they suffer because most of the time their demands are not met. Then they start complaining that life has turned against them and that it is all other people's fault. The life of the narcissist depends on gratification. They have to continuously succeed in order to feel good about themselves. But no one gets to live the perfect life. Everyone's existence is fraught with uncertainty.

Part 4.3

So many are disgusted by the psychiatric illness because they see it has something that society negatively labels. A huge component of the malady is that society in general stigmatizes those that have severe mental illness. If the individual suffering is narcissistic, this complicates things further. Only can the sufferer mature when they accept their illness as part of them and as part of their response to society. As RD Laing suggested, psychiatric illness can be breakdown or break-through - it all depends on one's mentality. The way to conquer your psychiatric illness is to embrace it as part of you.

What happens usually though is the use their psychiatric illness to justify why they are failing at life in comparison to others. "If only I wasn't mentally ill, then my life would be better." This is self-pity and self-pity is the most toxic emotional one can possess. Self-pity will make you miserable and unhappy. Such an individual then turns to the consultants and orders them to make them (the individual) happy. When that does not materialize, they then blame the doctors for failing their duties. I recall a woman who said she lost ten years of her life to mental illness. The tragedy was that she would lose the next ten as well, unless she changed her attitude. It was not mental illness that ruined her life - it was her perspective. If only she could learn to accept her malady as part of her, then she could be grateful. Life, as Soren Kierkegaard said, can only be understood backwards but must be lived forwards. A pity the woman in question did not abide by this quote.

Self-pity is a product of the capitalistic environment we inhabit. Such a sufferer has been raised to demand love, a good career, lots of friends, a nice house and car, and so on, as the means to be happy. When they don't attain these things, they then wallow in self-pity and start blaming everything but themselves. "If only that had not happened, then I would be successful; if only I wasn't disabled, then I would be successful." Such individuals are all the time yearning for more and take their actual existence in this universe for granted. What they need is a therapist to pull them out of their diseased mentality. As the saying goes you either get bitter or you get better - gratitude is a most potent venom, if only they realized this.

Part 5.1

Gratitude is the key to changing your life. Gratitude is the opposite and the antidote to narcissism. Those that are extremely narcissistic completely lack any sense of gratitude. Thus they continue to stumble in life, oblivious to where they are going wrong. Gratitude and narcissism are indirectly proportional to each other - as one goes up the other goes down and vice versa. Gratitude can be considered a personality trait just as narcissism is a personality disorder - it is a whole mentality and it immediately improves your life.

But to be grateful you must invite solitude into your life. Most are so toxic because they are seldom alone in this world. They are always mingling with others, be it the community or the work-place. The group makes one diseased; it corrupts us. In that we live-for-others rather than live-for-oneself. That is why we are materialistic and utterly consumed with ambition - the group. Thus to mature you must spend time alone and think for yourself and question what you are doing. This is essentially what a therapist tries to fulfil when you meet him or her for an hour a week. They are trying to get you to think for once in your life.

Once you start seeing the beauty of existence you will become mature. You must gaze into the stars at night and wonder why there is a universe and not a universe? Where did we all come from? Why are the laws of physics the way they are? How did the first cell come into existence? One must always think of how lucky they are to be alive, even when life is most difficult. Nothing hits you as hard in life as life itself - we all have our own unique burdens. But you must find some solace in the pain and suffering. Where there is life, there is hope. You must see this.

The End

You can read much more about this in greater detail in my self-help book: "Remarks On Existential Nihilism: Labelling, Narcissism and Existential Maturity."

You can also read more about labelling in my second book on the theory: "The Labelling Phenomenon: Volume Two."

Lightning Source UK Ltd.
Milton Keynes UK
UKHW010912080223
416610UK00014B/1470